Arjun Singh

Ancient art and architectural heritage of Jammu region

GRIN Publishing

Bibliographic information published by the German National Library:

The German National Library lists this publication in the National Bibliography;
detailed bibliographic data are available on the Internet at http://dnb.dnb.de .

Imprint:

Copyright © 2014 GRIN Verlag GmbH
Print and binding: Books on Demand GmbH, Norderstedt Germany
ISBN: 978-3-656-86010-5

This book at GRIN:

http://www.grin.com/en/e-book/285860/ancient-art-and-architectural-heritage-of-
jammu-region

GRIN - Your knowledge has value

Since its foundation in 1998, GRIN has specialized in publishing academic texts by students, college teachers and other academics as e-book and printed book. The website www.grin.com is an ideal platform for presenting term papers, final papers, scientific essays, dissertations and specialist books.

Visit us on the internet:

http://www.grin.com/

http://www.facebook.com/grincom

http://www.twitter.com/grin_com

ANCIENT ART AND ARCHITECTURAL HERITAGE OF JAMMU REGION

Dr. Arjun Singh

Assistant Professor, Chanderprabhu Jain College of Higher Studies & School of Law, Narella. (Affiliated to Guru Govind Singh Indraprastha University, Delhi)

The art and architecture disseminated to the other parts of India and the region of Jammu did not lag behind as compare to other art and architecture of the cultural material. The remnants of art and architecture, coins and tools, as well as other archaeological objects, which have been discovered in appreciable quantities, serve as first hand pictorial and material sources for the ancient cultural history of Jammu region. The culture of the people of Jammu region has been blended out of diverse elements, both indigenous and exotic. This culture has its roots in the pre-historic modes of primitive human society, growing through various stages of evolution and enriched and polished by numerous tribes and communities entering the region from abroad and from within India. The traditions of culture, art and architecture, religion, craft folk art spontaneously flow uninterrupted from the popular activities of the past. The past generations of Jammu region seem to have left behind a rich legacy of all such socio-cultural aspects.

(i). TRADITIONS IN ARCHITECTURE

The achievements of the people of Jammu in the sphere of art and architecture may be assessed from the remains of a variety of monuments in various stages of existence ranging from crumbling debris to fresh robust structures of the 18th and 19th centuries, which lies scattered in Jammu region. The earliest extant archaeological remains go back to as early as period of 9th and 10th centuries A.D.[1] In Jammu region, temples form the chief wealth of architecture and in their evolution, we discover two rounds which exhibits ancient stone structures of *śikhara* type was prevalent all over northern India during 8th-9th centuries A.D. Secondly, brick structures with thin tapering lofty *śikharas* and *pradakṣinā* belong to the later, eighteenth and nineteenth century[2]. During the intervening period no temple structure worth the name were raised or at least have not been discovered so far, which sounds a strange phenomenon in the history of evolution of Jammu architecture. It may have been mostly due to the absence of architectural activity in this region because of recurring foreign inroads and the vandalism of invaders from the thirteenth century onwards until the death of Aurangzeb.

(ii). STONE TEMPLES OF ANCIENT PERIOD

Main features of ancient stone temples

These types of temples are entirely made of stone and are usually decorated with carvings, its conical spire or *śikhara* form that peculiarly is technically designed as the *śikhara* or a square cella, a small portico and a low platform. In the developed form a covered ambulatory or *pradakshinā* and a low tower is seen added to the original concept. In the centuries to follow more improvements and additions were made as a result of the gusto of building activities during the early middles ages and it attained a definite and well laid down concept and came to consist of the following structural design, *śaili.*

(a). The *vimāna* or the shrine

(b). The *antrāla* or vestibule

(c). The *maṇdapa* or the assembly hall

(a). The vimāna or the shrine

The *vimāna* is main structure, which contains inside the *garbhagṛha* housing the idol of the deity to whom the temple is dedicated. The *vimāna* is surmounted by a high tapering tower called the *śikhara,* which in case of ancient structures is rendered somewhat circular in shape and curvilinear in case of temples of later centuries, both type being topped by an *amalaka* in some form crowned by a *kalasa* (finial), or only *amalaka* which is circular ribbed stone disk. The *garabhagṛhā* is dark, the only natural light it has is which enters it through its door from the *maṇdapa .*[3] A lamp is usually kept lighted, symbolic of the divine power illuminating the mysterious universe.

(b). The antrāla or vestibule

The *garbhagṛha* is joined to the *maṇdapa through* the *antrāla* i.e. a small vestibule.

(c) The maṇdapa or the assembly hall

The *maṇdapa* is a pillared hall where the devotees gather to worship the deity. The outer door of the *maṇdapa* is sometime covered by a small verandah or porch called *ardha-maṇdapa, which* serves as the entrance portico and is in some cases open on all the three side, supported by two or four pillars in front. The *śikhara* type covered *pradakṣinā-path* or

2

circumambulatory passage for going round the *garabhagṛhā*, emanating from the left side of the *antrāla* and merging in it on the opposite side. This is to say the modified modern *śikhara* style, a result of the introduction of brick as the construction material.[4]

(iii). ANCIENT TEMPLES OF JAMMU REGION

In Jammu region, *śikhara* temples both of ancient and recent origin are very common. These vary in this regard to, as they possess only the sanctuary or more parts of a typical *śikhara* temple. Some of the temple consist of a single cella in which the idol is housed and have an enter room or *maṇdapa*. The ancient temples, however, entered through an ornamented porch usually supported by two pillars. From outside the early medieval temples in Jammu region are two types.

(i).   Firstly, *ṭṛiratha* embellished by a variety of carvings and architectural designs as in the case of temples at Krimachi and most probably the Devi shrine at Babour.

(ii).   The second type to be seen in all other temples at Babour, which are not *ṭṛiratha* in construction but are equally decorated with carved embellishments and architectural design.

The temple of recent origin do not posses such outer formalities except that they have large curvilinear *śikharas* with a small melon-type *amalaka* or simply a *bhumi* in some cases on the highest narrow point to serve as base for a metallic *kalaśa*, set of three *ghāṭās* diminishing upwards, topped by a lotus bud pointed upwards. The lower portion or *janghā* is invariably a rectangular construction, all constructed out of bricks, leaving no scope for carved embellishment, but only for architectural designs, embellishing niches, projections like eves, *bandhanas, ardha- śikharas* and the like.

Approximately all around the city of Jammu there exist a number of ancient temples almost all of them are built in *śikhara*[5] style.

(a). KRIMCHI GROUP OF TEMPLES

About sixty km. from Jammu and 10 km from Udhampur on the north-west ranges, Ladhā is an ancient place of Krimchi, now merely a hamlet of a few huts, it was once a famous capital of Bhutyal[6] regime. It is situated on the bank of Birunala,[7] which flows on the east side of the town. It was known earlier as Bhutesvari[8] River and is still known by that name to the temple priest of that temple which is still under worship.

When we attempt to reconstruct early history of Krimchi particularly of the period to which the temples belong, we find that there are not reliable sources of information to be used as the basis. However, a few oral accounts and legends give some information about the place. The local people of the region say that the Raja Kichaka, a warrior of *Mahābhārata* period laid the foundation of Kirmchi.[9] Krimchi temples, according to the residents of the village, were erected by the Pāndva[10] brothers while in exile, Yudhishthira and his brothers lived incognito at the court of Raja Virāta of *Matsyadeśa*.[11] As per the style of the architecture the temples resembles with Bhuvaneśvara group of temples and Paraśurāmeśvara temple. As is well known during the period, Bhuvaneśvara group of temples belong to regional variations within the *Nāgara*[12] style of temples. The architectural style of the edifices point out the possibility of their construction during the eighth or ninth century A.D.[13]

In this context it should be noted that by the time of 8th - 9th century A.D. various texts dealing with temple architecture were composed. Few *śilpaśāstras* were composed in Orissian region and therefore we find a different terminology related with the various components of temples applicable to that region alone. For example, if components of fully developed temples are known at Khajuraho as *Ardha- mandapa, mandapa, mahāmandapa and garbhagrha*.[14] They are known in Bhuvaneśvara as *bhoga mandapa, natamandapa, jagamohana* and *deul*.[15]

The Krimchi groups of temples belong to *Nāgara* style of temple architecture, which was popular in Orissa. Therefore, we have adopted the technical terminology in Orissian canons of architecture.

(1).   The temple No. 1 is most intact in composition when compared with other temples of this group. It stands on the same platform on which all other temples except temple no. 5 are situated. The temple possesses *Jagamohana*, vestibule and deul. From inside *Jagamohana* is square in plan and measures 5'-0" x 5'-0".[16] For the entrance door to *Jagamohana* and foliated do not suggest that it possessed any more components adjoining to it. Moreover, therefore, whatsoever type of construction preceded *Jagamohana* it was constructed in latter days. The ground plan of present remains is simple. The deul is approaches by a vestibule. From inside vestibule is square in plan and it measures 4'-0" x 4'-0". The deul is small and it is square in plan and measure 7'-0" x 7'-0". From outside the deul is *triratha* in plan and possessed the usual features of Orissan group of temples. It is divided into several *pagas* by the projection in *bada* and these *pagas* are carried up to the *beki*. In elevation, the deul contain all the features known to Orissan style of architecture. There are niches carved with beautiful motifs with overflowing flower petals and other structures in the temples.

(2). **The temple No. 2** is situated on the same platform adjoining to the temple no. 1. The temple possesses *Jagamohan*, vestibule and duel. From inside *Jagamohan* is square and it measures 21'-00" x 21'-0". The *Jagamohan* has three entrance doors- one in front. All the three entrance doors to the *Jagamohana* rest on four pillars. Each pillar has 16 inside shaft. These pillars have square base and above the base, there is round molding followed by the shaft of the pillar. Main ornamentation is at the top where we have one ornamental band followed by two moldings. We have on all four faces the *ghata* motifs with overflowing flower petals.

The *Jagamohan* leads to deul through a vestibule. From inside, it is rectangular in plan and it measures 4'-0" x 5'-6". From outside it is *triratha* [17] in plan.

(3). **The temple No. 3** is situated at a plane little higher than those of no. 1 and 2. It is simple in construction and resembles with temple no. 1. The temple possesses *Jagamohana*, vestibule and *garbhagriha*. The temple is entered through a small porch, which has been constructed keeping in view *Jagamohana*.

The *Jagamohana* is a small essential component of temple architecture of the period to which the groups belong. From inside, *Jagamohana* is rectangular in plan and it measures 8'-6" x 5'-0". From outside it carries similar to that temple no. 1. However, due to use of decorative motifs it differs slightly. It carries gable shaped roof but decoration of door lintel and gable is altogether different from the temple no. 1. The *sikhara* of the *Jagamohan* is mutilated but it provides the idea about the construction. On the side walls there are niches type projection having gable shaped roof. The deul is approaches by a vestibule. From inside it is square in plan and it measures 3'-6" x 3'-6" from outside it is *triratha* in plan. It is divided into several *pagas* by the projection of *bada*. However, since on all the three sides on the *rāhapagas* there are niches having gable shaped *sikharas*, which were meant to enshrine gods and goddesses. It is interesting to note that each niche has a small deul and Jagamohana. [18]

(4).   The temple No. 4 is situated on the same platform and faces temple no. 2. Thus, its entrance is from west. The shrine consists of a small *antarāla* and the sanctum. From inside, *antarāla* is rectangular in plan and it measure 5'-0" x 3'-6". The *antarāla is* enters through a door bigger in size than that of deul. From inside it is also square in plan. It measures 5'-2" x 5'-2" on the left wall of the sanctum. There is a water outlet is of a typical shape common to śaiva shrines from *nirmalya* used to flow.[19]

(5).   The temple No. 5 is located adjoining to the water stream which used to flow earlier to the east of present temple complex. It is perhaps the earliest construction of the group and therefore was near rivulet. The temple consists of *Jagamohana,* vestibule and deul. From inside, it is rectangular in plan and its measures 8'-9" x 11'-0". It appears from the present remains, *Jagamohana* have been constructed with the help of pillars. From outside there are traces of niches which is common in all the intact temples of group. The deul is approaches by vestibule. From inside the vestibule is rectangular in plan and it measures 2'-0" x 3'-6". From outside, the deul is *ṭriratha* in plan. From inside it is square in plan and it measures 8'-0" x 8'-0". It has made feasible to know the technique employed to the construction of *śikhara.* From the certain traces of the back portion of the temple, it is suggested that there were decorative motifs on the *rāhapagas.*[20]

(6).   Brick wall: During the course of conservation work at Krimchi, Archaeological Survey of India encountered a brick wall. The wall, which was running in east-west direction and measuring 30 meters long and 1½ meter high, was found. This wall was found side hidden inside the temple platform on the southern side. To ascertain the actual nature of the brick wall and its relation with the temple building activity, the brick structure was thoroughly exposed and its extent was traced by lying trenches further south of the brick wall. In all, four trenches were laid and in all the squares, irregular bricks at floor ascribe to the Gupta period era encountered. The major portion of the floor level was either found missing or robbed. In the course of exposition of flooring and the brick wall, a good number of molded bricks, triangular and wedge-shape bricks were also uncounted. The standard size of bricks available is 6 x12 x 24 cms. The above discoveries and the find indicate that the temple building activity started at Kirmchi sometime in the 4th -5th century A.D.[21] During the course of this small excavation, terracotta human and animal figurines, terracotta areca nut shaped beads, balls dabbers, iron arrowheads, nails, chisels and circular and rectangular copper coins[22] were found.

REFERENCES

1. Charak S.D.S.& Billawaria Anita , *History and Culture of Himalayan States. Vol. VIII,* Jammu, 1997, p.33.

2. *Ibid.,* p.33.

3. *Ibid.,* p.34

4. *Ibid.,* pp.34-35.

5. Jerath Ashok, *Hindu Shrines of the Western Himalayas,* Jammu, 2001, p. 9.

6. *Ibid.*

7. Billawaria Anita, *Ancient Temples of Krimchi,* Jammu, 1991, p. 1.

8. *Ibid.*

9. Balauria Th. Kahan Singh, *Tarikh-i-Rajaputana-i-Mulk Punjab,* p. 415.

10. Jerath Ashok, *op.cit,* p. 10.

11. Roy P.C., The *Mahabharta* (English translation), Vol. IV, p. 9.

12. Billawaria Anita, *op.cit,* p. 18.

13. Charak S.S., *History and Culture of Himalayan States, Vol. VI.* Delhi, 1988, p. 75.

14. Brown Percy, *Indian Architecture,* 3rd ed. Bombay, 1956, p. 110.

15. *Ibid.*

16. Billawaria Anita, *op.cit,* p. 20.

17. *Ibid.,* p. 26.

18. *Ibid.,* pp. 27-28.

19. *Ibid.,* p. 29.

20. *Ibid.,* pp. 30-31.

21. *Indian Archaeology, A Review.* 1989-90, p. 33.

22. *Ibid.*